The Aisle
The Story of How I Met My Wife

Vincent Hope

TANZANIA EDUCATIONAL PUBLISHERS LTD

Tanzania Educational Publishers Ltd,
TEPU House,
Uganda road, Plot No. 45 Block MDA,
Telephone: +255 685 997583/ +255 758 147871
Email: tepultd@yahoo.com
Website: www.tepu.co.tz
P.O. Box 1222,
Bukoba, Tanzania.

ISBN 978-9987-07-065-7

Dedication

This book is dedicated to My Lovely Wife

Deborah Nanchin Vincent

It's been a blessing Meeting and Walking with You in This Journey of Life. Together We Have Shared This Learning Process.

And

To our children: Angel Eunice, Joy and Anita

Thanks

I thank the Almighty God for the inspiration given to me to write this book.

Contents

The Story of How I Met My Wife

1. Going Back

I grew up as the son of a military personnel who served in the Nigerian Air force. And because of this, I spent some part of my teenage life and the early part of my adult life in the military barracks.

I can't speak for the rest of Africa, but in Nigeria, the time between early adulthood which starts from 18 years till the time you graduate from the University, is spent in the home of your parents.

Since I and my siblings had been raised up as people of faith, we went to church regularly.

It was a small church which was then located within the Air-force base. The base which is where the main air-force flying operations took place is directly opposite the barracks where the air force personnel lived.

You had to take between 10 to 15 minutes' walk from the barracks to get to the church.

This church was attended mainly by air force personnel and their families, and some other civilians who were either close associates of the personnel or had a conviction to worship at the center.

Since it was such a small church, almost every young person was involved in its activities.

The same could be said of the barracks. The air force barracks was well laid out, built in blocks of two flats each, with the next block only a stone throw away.

So, everyone lived as close neighbours and knew each other quite well. So, when a new family member or relative came visiting, he or she was quickly identified.

2. New Neighbours

It was a tradition in the air force and I believe in the military in general, that every year, fresh postings took place. Military personnel where moved to new locations across the country, depending on the area of need, skill-set and rank.

This fateful year, the postings where done and we had new neighbours coming into the flat, three blocks away.

In time, I began to notice from that house, a friendly, jovial but very hardworking woman. She was a teacher working at the air-force primary school, and came on posting with her husband, who was an air-force personnel.

At the early stage I didn't notice him, because he was always out to work and I was also in school and came back home in the evenings. But, I could not, but notice his wife who, as I said, was very hardworking.

The air-force base which was still being developed at the time, had several large expanses of unused land, which the residents used for farming.

I noticed that this woman, our new neighbour, was always on the farm during the rainy season, cultivating the land, weeding and harvesting. She alone cultivated large portions of land and her harvest, as I came to know later, were very huge.

In time, her first son who had just completed his diploma in accounting, returned to stay with them. Because we all went to the same church and he is very good in music, he and my junior brother who was also in the choir became good friends.

He visited our home regularly and my brother also visited him at home. From there, the relationship grew between both families. Most times, if you wanted to know the whereabouts of my brother, you only needed to check the home of Moses – that is his name.

3. My First Glimpse of Her

I heard of it – the younger sister of Moses is around. She had just completed her diploma and came back home to stay with her parents.

Since I was not very close to Moses personally, it really wasn't of much interest to me. At that time I was running my degree programme at Bayero University Kano, and still held a job at an ICT firm as a computer instructor.

After some days, from the balcony of my house, I noticed a young lady who I had not seen before, walking to one of the blocks, I think, to see a neighbour or purchase an item from one of the several homes that sold home supplies in small kiosks setup in front of their house.

She had a low cut, dressed very simply and seemed to be moving very fast as if she had spring in her steps. My first impression of her was that she was just a normal, young lady, nothing special or unusual.

Honestly at first glance, she didn't strike me as beautiful, maybe because her hair was undone or she didn't fit into the – tall, slim and fair lady picture, most young men of my age had of their dream girls.

4. Meeting Her

In time she and my younger brother became good friends, because he was always going to their house to see Moses his friend and secondly she also joined the church choir.

Because of this, she started coming to our home to see my younger brother. I think on the first day we met, which I can't vividly, remember now, we just exchanged pleasantries, talked a little and that was it.

Sometimes the barracks would experience water shortages, which could be due to lack of electricity to pump water from the central water system or due to a fault in its operations.

Because of this fault, the water could not be pumped into the various homes, so the children from each block had to proceed to a central reservoir still located within the barracks to fetch water for domestic use.

This usually happened in the evenings, when everyone had come back from school and work. This was an excellent time for the young people within the barracks to interact and spend time together.

At these times she and my younger brother will go together to the central reservoir, with a hand wheeled water carriage to fetch water.

Because these times were times for interactions, the young people spent a longer time than was necessary.

Another factor that enhanced interactions between young people was going to church. Almost every young person participated actively in church activities, from the children choir, to prayer team, children department etc.

So, anytime my younger brother was going to church, his first point of call was the house of Moses and his younger sister.

5. Her Name is Debra

Her elder brother's name was Moses and she was called Deborah. She usually introduced herself as Debra a more fun and cool way to call it.

She had another native name called **Nanchin**. In Nigeria every person had a religious name and a native name.

Native names were used to identify from which part of the country you came from. It was also used to convey a meaning that the parents wanted to express, such as an expression of joy, hope, peace or victory. For example **Nanchin** means **God's Gift**.

Another very noticeable feature she had is her angelic voice. Every time she speaks, heads will turn to see who she was. I remember once, while we were in church and she stood up to read the bible, even while I knew it was her reading, I couldn't resist but to turn to be sure who was her reading.

Her voice is very soft, sweet and pleasant to listen to. When she speaks, it is like music to your ears. You will want her to speak more. Her voice is so distinct that she almost sounds like an American.

Another striking feature of her voice, was that it was completely different from the rest of her siblings. Nobody spoke like that in her home. Some say it was because of this melodious voice of hers that I was attracted to her – well I think it was part of it - (*laugh*).

Her voice was not only the sweet part of her. Her personality is also amazing. Once you are with her and start a conversation, you will want to tell her everything about yourself. This is not an exaggeration.

Not one or two or three, but several people over the course of time I have known her even up till this day, people who just met her for the very first time, will tell her at a sitting the history or story of their lives.

Overtime I have come to discover that this is a special gift that the Almighty God bestowed on her; a gift where everyone wants to share themselves with her, even their deepest selves. I think you will also do so when you meet with her.

She is very warm, interesting and fun to be with. There is never a dull moment with her. She is never at loss of words, topics or ideas to discuss or gist about. One of the reasons I believe is responsible for her versatility in life issues, was her early exposure to reading from a very young age.

She told me that as young as five, she used to sit with her dad to read newspapers and listen to the news, even when she didn't understand much of what she read.

This love for reading progressed to reading of books and novels. She once stayed with a family that had a library, which she took advantage of and expanded her world of books. In-fact in the early stages of our relationship, I learnt so much from her which I am very grateful for up till this day.

She is also a very outgoing person. She is not reserved in anyway. She likes to go out, visit friends and connect. She loves people. She takes keen interest in meeting people, knowing them, sharing with them and touching their lives in a very significant way. Once you have had a moment with her, you will want to have many more moments with her.

She is also very warm. For everyone she meets, she gives you more than a handshake, she gives you a hug. She wants you to always feel loved and at ease in her presence.

Her smile is also inviting. Her laughter is very funny. When she laughs, she lets loose and just laughs. Sometimes her laughter can be so loud that you have to tell her to tone it down.

Her smiles, laughter, warmth and friendliness will make you think she is shy and timid. But this is far from it. She is very bold and most times to an uncomfortable level.

She can look you straight into the eyes and tell you what she doesn't like. She is not afraid to confront people when she feels strongly that she needs to.

She is also a person of faith. She deeply believes in God, and expresses this in every of her words and conduct. She is regular in church and loves fellowshipping with her brethren.

Debra is all of this in one package. I will leave you to your imagination.

6. Her Relationship(s)

As she visited our home regularly, our interactions grew. I started visiting her at her home and she would talk and talk and entertain me with gist.

In time, I came to find out that she was in a relationship with a guy she seemed to like very much. She always told me he was tall, handsome and at that time in the seminary, training to be a pastor and I think she liked the idea of marrying a pastor.

She told me she met him in one of the outreach programmes that was embarked on by the ministry she was a member of. The pastor in charge of the ministry regularly held outreach programmes to reach people with the gospel of Christ.

She was part of the small choir group that ministered on every occasion during this programme. On one of the occasions she met this guy and according to her she was swept of her feet – I wonder why she is still standing (*Laugh*).

They started dating. She would go to visit him in the seminary, where he will proudly introduce her to his colleagues. They will talk for hours, about everything including plans for marriage.

He took her to his parents, introduced her to his uncle and relatives and things where going on just fine.

As at the time I met her, they had dated for about two years and the guy had already proposed marriage to her and was making moves to come to see her parents.

At this stage she started nursing some fears, as to whether she really wanted to settle down in marriage with him. She shared those fears with me, along with the differences she observed they had that made them not compatible.

I honestly advised her the best way I could then on what she could do to fix the relationship and advance into marriage. She still wasn't convinced. At that time they were having a strain in the relationship and things were not as smooth as before.

While this was going on, there was another guy in her choir much older than her, with whom she had grown much fond off. The guy let's call him Fred, did not like the relationship she had developed with the pastor in training. One reason was because he too was interested in her.

Eventually the relationship with the pastor in training was dissolved. Then Fred now officially expressed his love for her. He told her he had been interested in her, but was waiting for the right moment to make it known to her.

Fred was the leader of the choir or band which she belonged to. He was also a degree student of the same university which she attended. They had been singing together in the band for about two years, they went everywhere together, and both of them had grown fond of each other.

So, when he expressed his love to her, it was hard for her to refuse. The relationship between them was brief and could not grow, one of the reason being that they were now far apart, she was now in Kano and he was in Jos.

7. It Grew

The more we shared the more our relationship grew. We started to get fond of ourselves. She will visit me regularly, we talked, laughed and continued to gist.

She would buy me gifts. I remember on one occasion she bought me three (3) sweets and wrapped in a short love letter. She parcelled it to me through my cousin brother.

I had just returned from work and was not expecting anything. Then my cousin brother gave me the parcel and told me who it was from – Nanchin.

It was exciting for me. I felt liked, loved and cared for. I opened it, read the contents of the letter and ate the sweets with much joy. The words in the letter sent love chills down my system and made me wanted to see her.

I had just bought my first personal computer and brought it home. This was also exciting for me. That evening, while I was working on it and after I had received the parcel, she came visiting.

I was very excited to see her. After thanking her for her gift, we talked and talked and talked. It was an exciting day.

In the evenings, when it was time to fetch water from the central reservoir system, I would be excited to go just because it will be an ample opportunity to be with her.

We preferred to take a walk, pushing the truck of

water, so we would have time to talk and share everything that happened in the day.

On one occasion we took a walk close to the primary school located within the barracks. We sat on the road engrossed in our discussions. Unknown to us the school premises was being patrolled by a soldier on duty, because thieves had broken into the school a day before.

He accosted us and asked for explanations of what we were doing there at the school premises at that time. We tried to explain that we were children of soldiers in the barracks, but, because he was drunk, he refused to listen.

He harassed us with his gun and even hit me with it. We pleaded with him, but, he was adamant and took me to the air-police office to explain myself.

Deborah quickly went to inform my dad about what was happening, who came swiftly to the air-police station to take me home. He was visibly angry and showed it.

But this incident did not stop us from seeing each other, but it made us more careful.

She started visiting me in my office. When she came we would talk and talk and talk. Sometimes she came visiting in the office and we went home together. On one occasion, I held a seminar in my office and lacked some items to put it together. When I told her about it, she was all over the place seeing what she could do to help.

On some occasions, I took her out to a popular ice cream center that offered various ice creams and snacks and we just ate, talked and had a good time. At this time we were officially dating.

8. The Competition

While all this was happening, there was this other guy let's call him Paul, who was a friend of her elder brother Moses.

Paul attended the same secondary school with Moses, and when they met in Kano, their relationship blossomed. He lived in an estate that was about 15 minutes' walk from the barracks.

He was a graduate, had a cool and calm personality and also a person of faith. He had a good job and lived in his own rented house and was doing well. At the time I was still living in my parents' house.

Moses would regularly visit Paul at his residence and sometimes he went with Debra. He also visited Moses in the barracks and the interactions between him and Debra also grew.

He became fond of her and in time secretly fell in love with her but did not disclose this to her.

She had a hint that he did, but was not also sure about it. When it became obvious that we had taken our relationship to the next level i.e. began to talk about marriage, he disclosed to her his intentions.

She apologized and told him it was too late.

9. God's Call

It was the last quarter of the year 1999, and as final year students of the university, we were all preparing and writing our final exams.

The exams spanned between two to three weeks depending on the courses of choice. For us in the mathematics department, we had to prepare hard, to ensure we scaled through.

As students, we organized tutorial sessions amongst

ourselves, to deepen our understanding of what had been taught. In these tutorial sessions, those with deeper understanding of the subject matter, shared their knowledge, while others asked questions.

For me, since I was still working and schooling at the same time, I could only attend some of the tutorial sessions.

So far, we had all made substantial progress in the exams, and on this day we were all putting finishing touches to write our final paper.

I was sitting alone, on my desk trying to memorize some mathematical formulas, when I heard a loud voice in my ears with these words - *rephrased* - **"It is time to get married".**

First, I knew it was the Voice of God, because he had been speaking to me on several occasions, over the years now.

Secondly, I knew who he wanted me to get married to, because I had been dating Debra for a while now, but it still came as a shocker to me, because frankly speaking at that time I was not ready.

All through the time I wrote that final paper, I

was thinking about what I had just heard. Several questions arose in my mind:

i. How was I going to achieve this?

ii. I didn't have any money.

iii.I had a job, but the pay was not enough to sustain a marriage.

iv. I don't have an apartment of my own; I was still living in my parents' house.

I finished the paper and as I was going home, these questions and many more, kept going through my mind.

10. Making the First Move

While thinking about these questions, I came up with strategies I believed would align me on that path. The first was obviously to tell her of my intentions.

At this time our love had grown strong. We had talked a lot about our future together, but I had not officially proposed to her.

She was also in the process of going back to the university, for her degree programme.

I remember that night quite well. It was normal day, but different for me, because I had been rehearsing all day, on how I was going to put it forward to her i.e. how I was going to propose marriage to her.

I remember that so many ideas ran through my head, was I going to use the American style - bow my knees and give a ring and pop the question would you marry me – (*Laugh*). My heart was pumping fast, as if there was a continuous flow and rush of blood through my entire body.

That night I sent for her. After a while she came dressed in a brown long sleeved light wool sweater on top of a skirt, wearing her glasses, and in a very warm and calm disposition.

She came staring at me, as if she knew what I was going to say, and I popped those famous words to her; **WOULD YOU MARRY ME** and she said **YES**.

I hugged her and we were both excited. I can't remember now whether I was able to sleep that night, but what I can honestly say was that I was full of joy.

11. The Hurdles

Nigeria is made up of several ethnic groups who have different languages and cultures. When it comes to a serious institution like marriage, people prefer to marry those from their ethnic group because of the similarities of culture, custom and language.

Parents felt safe that their daughters were close by, by marrying men from their own tribes who they understood their customs and ways of thinking.

It was believed that a woman married to a man from another culture was going to face a lot of difficulties, adjusting to his customs and traditions.

Stories abound of how women married off to other tribes, were subjected to harsh realities of customs and traditions which they were not prepared for.

Many cross cultural marriages did take place in Nigeria, most were very successful and some had sad tales to tell.

For us we had a church setting. As people of faith we believed that the bond of our faith was far stronger than our cultural affiliations. This was consistently taught and preached in church and as such we had so many successful cross cultural marriages in church because they were of the same faith.

After that night, assured that I had gotten a definite commitment from her. I took the next step. All this while I went to visit her at her home, I was well received and had had several interactions with her parents. Her dad was friendly but quiet and didn't talk much. Her mum on the other hand was very jovial and more interactive. And I think she did like my person.

Based on that perception, I felt that the first person to tell of my intentions to marry Debra outside both of us was her mum.

One faithful morning, when I knew she was at home, because her dad had travelled, I summoned courage and knocked on the door, she opened the door and welcomed me in. I told her about my intentions to marry her daughter, which she listened with rapt attention.

When I was done she told me she was going to think about it and relay it to her dad.

This was the beginning of the many hurdles to come. I later realized that all this while her mother saw our relationship as a joke, a fantasy that was not going to have any future.

It seemed my going to inform her mother about my intentions of marrying Debra, triggered the unfriendly side of her, which was kept under wraps. Debra later told me that her mum found my coming to her offensive because it did not follow the usual customs and norms in the Nigerian Society – and I must admit she was right.

In Nigeria, when a guy is interested in a lady and intends to marry her, he does not go directly to her parents. He either informs his parents, who will directly make the first visit on his behalf or call in the services of an uncle who will act as a middle man or intermediary between his parents and the parents of the bride to be.

First the middle man along with another relative of the groom to be, **Knocks** (that is what it is called) or approaches the parents of the bride to be, to inform them of the intention of the groom to be. They must go with at least a bottle of wine, kola-nuts and sometimes garden egg fruit.

They pre-inform the parents of the bride to be and on the set date, usually in the evening, they come and make their intentions known.

The parents of the girl receive them, listen to their intentions and asks for a later date in order to seek the consent of the girl and consult with other relatives, to commence the marriage rights.

All this was not done. The first reason was because I did not know about it, secondly I did not consult with my dad and thirdly I was in love and just wanted to go on with it.

Another contentious issue, her mother raised, was the fact that I was still living under the roof of my parents. Any serious minded man that was going to settle down in marriage, should have a house of his own.

This information prompted me to begin the search for an apartment of my own, although I was already contemplating that even before I finished my final exams. I later settled down in a flat which I shared with a very close friend of my mine who I looked up to as an elder brother.

But this was amongst the many hurdles that came. I informed my dad of my intentions to marry Debra and urged him to do the needful customs and rights to get the process going.

These things don't happen in day, so time went by. All this time I was still going to the house to visit her, but the reception was no longer the same. When I greeted her mum, she would answer me pleasantly, but I could see through the smiles that – I was not welcomed.

Deborah would tell me how in several discussions, her mum would disapprove of my person, as not been qualified to marry her. And this often led to disagreements and quarrels between both of them.

At a point she told her that I didn't even earn enough to take care of her, after she secretly got information on how much I was earning at that time, which still amazes me up-till today, how she got to know about it.

Eventually my dad made moves and paid the first official visit to her parents to officially inform them of my intentions to marry Debrah.

They were well received and a close relative of theirs was brought into the picture to act as their own middle man between their family and ours, in order to smoothen the process. This was tradition.

But this didn't calm the situation, it seemed to have escalated it. The disapprovals from the mum did not stop. The disagreements and quarrels between Debrah and her mother because of me, increased.

Her dad who was away on training, came back and was briefed. Her mother did a lot to convince the dad that I was not the right kind of husband for their daughter.

Debrah tried to convince him otherwise, but her mum's opinion was stronger. But he did love his daughter dearly.

To calm the situation, on one occasion when I received my salary, I went to a popular store in town and bought a lot of assorted items which includes biscuits, juice, sweets and packaged it and took it directly to the parents one evening. I could see they appreciated it.

As time progressed things didn't seem to get better. Tension grew in the home between Debrah and her mum.

One other reason I suspect, was the cause of this disagreement was because earlier, before the issue of marriage came up, my dad and her mum usually interacted.

My dad who was having a running battle of his own with my mum; they had their own quarrels and fights, and most times relayed the issue to Debra's mum. This continued for a while which I did not know off. So she had built up a perception of my family as one that always had issues to deal with and didn't want her daughter to be part of it.

The disagreements and quarrels between Debra and her mum got to a peak during one of my birthdays. She had bought me a nice shirt along with a card and packaged it to give it to me in the evening. When her mum got to see it, she took the gift and burnt it. You wouldn't believe it but that was what happened.

When I went to visit her that day and she told me about it, I didn't know what to make out of the situation. But, really I couldn't do anything about it, but just hoped and prayed for a change of heart on her part.

All this while I had continuous interactions with the relative of hers who served as their middle man. He was very helpful. He did his the best to convince the mum that our marriage was going to work out. His firm conviction came from his own story.

He was once in a relationship with a lady, whom he loved very much. Their love was so strong that they lived together for eight years and even had a son together. But, tradition and customs did not allow him to consummate the marriage with her.

He was the first son of his family and was compelled to marry from his tribe. His father at that time wouldn't want to hear that he was in love with a girl from another tribe. It came to a point when the father had to come to town where he was living with her and threw her belongings out of the house.

He was later given another wife from his tribe, who is married to today. That experience made him really give us his support. And he did a lot to help us.

Another side of the story came from the assistant pastor of the church whom we had grown up to know. He would send for me to see him on several occasions and relay to me all the complaints, her mother had leveled against me. I did my best to explain to him my own side of the story. On these occasions he would put the question straight to me – "despite all these challenges do you still think you want to go ahead with this marriage and my response will simply be an emphatic YES.

12. It Got to Me

Because of the continuous disagreements and quarrels between Debrah and her mother, coupled with the long litany of complaints and negative news I was hearing about her disapprovals, not to talk of the huge debate it had generated in my home and among my family members who got involved in the process, I got fed up.

One evening I called Debrah and told her since her mum was not in support of our marriage and was doing everything to frustrate it, **I-was-no-longer-interested**.

I struggled to put those words together, it was even difficult to say them out. There was no flow in my speech – it was difficult.

She looked at me in disbelief and took it as a joke. The expression on her face and her body language was like – *after all we have gone through together, you want to quit now.*

We sat down together for a while and talked. She didn't seem to take what I said seriously. And after a while I had to explain to her that I said that because I was tired of all the negative news I was hearing concerning her mum's disapprovals.

I saw in her eyes that she didn't want me to go and with that I had to retract the statement and resolved to fight for the love we had together.

One very important move I made that gave a boost to our cause, was the visit I paid to her mum's eldest brother, whom they all regarded as - **father**.

He is a well-educated man, schooled abroad, was a one-time commissioner of his state, well-travelled and was greatly responsible for his sibling's upbringing after their father's death and this included Debra's mum.

He held the family together and his counsel within the family is highly respected.

Every December, the entire maternal family members of Debrah came from different parts of the country to the village during Christmas to celebrate family re-union. These seven existing members of the family came along with all their children to feasts, drink and share – It was called **Club-7**.

This year was special because **ba-ba**, as he was called, was celebrating his birthday, so I travelled along with Debra and her siblings to see him. It was also an opportunity to meet with members of her extended family.

Debra informed me that if I got his support, it will make things a lot easier for us.

On the day of his birthday, Debra and I packaged a gift for him. Later that evening when the event was over, I went to see him and told him about my intentions. He asked me a few questions and was pleased with my person and gave his nod.

I later learnt Debra's mum relayed her fears to him but he was not convinced. With his nod, we went on with our preparations in full swing.

13. The Traditional Rights

All this process took a while. In fact it took us about two years of negotiations for both families to finally agree on the terms of the marriage.

A date was fixed for the traditional marriage and both families were working towards this date. Traditional marriages in Nigeria are very important; in fact some see it as the proper marriage. Most churches have even declined to wed couples until they were sure that the traditional marriage has been concluded.

The traditional marriage is very important, because this is when the parents of the bride finally release her to the groom and his family after the dowry has been paid.

Dowry is a token given to the parents of the bride, more or less a thank you gift from the groom and his family; appreciating the value of the bride and all the efforts and resources her parents have invested in her from her childhood to the point of marriage.

It usually consists of a certain specified cash gift, kola-nuts, and certain amount of food stuffs, livestock and drinks. Another very important aspect of the dowry, are traditional clothes and dressings that must be bought for the bride before she goes into the home of the groom.

A large box or set of boxes will be demanded; which has to be filled with local traditional ladies materials, some of which include sets of laces, wrappers, shoes, jewelry, perfumes etc.

The groom is also expected to purchase the dresses the bride's parents are to put on the day of the wedding.

The groom is given a list of these items sometimes three months to the date of the traditional rights or marriage, so he can gradually put them together. This list when aggregated in local currency, usually runs into hundreds of thousands.

Sometimes the groom is given the latitude to negotiate the content of the list and if he has a good middle man, the cost can be trimmed down significantly, but there are still no-go-areas i.e. items that he must be purchased. It is after the traditional marriage that a date is fixed for the church wedding.

Mine was no exception. The list was large and so was the cost. I was given the list about three months ahead of the time we planned to hold our wedding. We did put heads together with my dad on what were the necessary items to be bought and which could be negotiated lower.

After we arrived at what should be bought, I started putting together these items gradually, and ticked off from list every item purchased.

14. The Intrigues Continued

Even after the terms had been agreed and preparations for the traditional marriage were on, that didn't stop Debra's mum from doing all she could to stop it from happening.

It was as if she was coerced to accept the marriage between us, despite all the YES voices that had grown in support of our coming together.

I continued to get feelers that she was not satisfied, with our future union together and did everything to discredit it at every opportunity.

The quarrels and disagreements between her and Debra had greatly reduced but it was not over. But she knew we were winning the battle.

15. The Traditional Wedding

The D-day finally arrived. Her relatives i.e. her father's siblings had been invited, had arrived and were at home, the day was full of high expectations.

Some hours before the time fixed i.e. 7 pm, all my relatives had also assembled at our house and a debate ensued among them on whether or not to proceed with the traditional rights based of the negative feelers they were still getting concerning the marriage.

Discussions went back and forth some called for a shift in the traditional marriage date to settle all things right, while other opted for a continuation.

I was asked to give my opinion on the matter and I insisted, that my future was at stake here and we all had to go along with it.

At the time set, I dressed up in traditional native attire and we all proceeded to the home of Debra.

Close friends of both myself and Debra and of both families were all there. Members of my family where still a bit on the edge based on all that have happened.

Her mum took on a very serious disposition. The first thing that was demanded was an inspection of the items presented to ensure that they were in line with the list given.

Her mum and the middle man appointed on their behalf took charge, and I was invited into one of their bedrooms along with a relative of mine to do the presentation.

The items were checked one after the other to ensure they were all available. Fortunately the most important items were available and the others that were not were negotiated.

After that was concluded, few speeches were made as way of introduction for the event and light refreshment was served to guests.

Debra was now invited. She was dressed beautifully in the same traditional attire I was wearing. The question was put across to her by the middle man representing her parents – **do you want to marry Hope** - and she said YES. This was followed by clapping, cheers and songs.

Refreshment consisting of Jollof rice and beef, a local rice delicacy in Nigeria, was served and everyone ate. This was followed by pictures of bride and groom along with the remaining guests.

The climax of the event was the prayer for the couple, which was offered by the assistant pastor of our local assembly, with me and Debra kneeling.

To confirm the fact that despite all these that has just happened, the mum was not still satisfied, her dad made a speech at the end of the ceremony which seemed to pour cold water on all the joy that was flowing from the event that night.

Even when he was speaking you could hear her mum in his voice – he said and I quote (rephrased) *"All that has happened here this night is not the real marriage."*

I could feel the chills of all those who were present. In my mind the question was if this was not marriage, what was it?

I knew that others had varied opinions of this response but they all held their peace.

For me and Debra that didn't matter much, the major hurdle had been crossed.

16. Church Wedding

After the traditional wedding, we picked a date for our church wedding, it was December 14th 2002. We started looking forward to it with excitement, a date when will finally come together forever as husband and wife and nothing to separate us.

We were really excited about this date because:

- We saw a great future together as a couple.

- It will be a celebration of victory for all the hurdles we had gone through, to be together.

Gradually the attitude of my new mother- in-law changed positively towards me, and it had to change because she had realized I was now her son-in-law and there was nothing she could do anymore to keep us apart.

She reverted to her old self which I once knew her with. She became jovial, friendly and fun to be with. But I still exercised great caution based on all that had happened.

The wedding plans went on well, I purchased most of what we needed for the wedding and we both made contacts to all those that needed to be informed.

A night before the wedding, we held a testimony night in the church, asked were we about how we met each other and were asked several questions especially from the young people.

On the wedding day, I was full of excitement.

It was a very beautiful day in which all the preparations for the marriage had climaxed.

Very early that day, preparations for cooking the main dish started.

Usually, in Nigeria the main dish for weddings is called *Jollof Rice,* which is actually white rice prepared with a mixture of palm oil, vegetables and spices, served with fried beef and salad.

The different processes for making the local delicacy was on. The rice was cooking, mashed tomatoes were on fire, the vegetables had been cut and assembled for mixture, so the whole environment was filled with the aroma of the dish.

On another end, the beef that was bought for the occasion – a cow, was been processed. Local beef processing specialists whose job was to kill and process the cow were busy doing their job. They killed the cow, removed the hide, and divided its parts into small pieces, so that it could be consumed by each person.

The whole place was full of activity, everybody doing one kind of chore or the other. I looked over a few blocks away, where the house of my fiancée was located and saw that there was a lot of activity also going on there.

People were moving in and out of the house, some going on errands and others busy with other chores.

All the inhabitants of the section of the military barracks where we were staying then knew that something good was in the air.

After going around to see what was happening to ensure that everything was going on smoothly, I went in to get ready for the wedding proper.

After dressing up, the motorcade that was arranged for the wedding, conveyed me and some of my family members to church, were we met my best men properly dressed and waiting and some church members had arrived, this was about 10 o'clock in the morning.

Not too long after that, my fiancée accompanied by her bride's maid and some family members arrived. She was beautifully dressed and full of smiles.

The wedding ceremony started in earnest, the activities were carried out and eventually our wedding was officiated. This as usual was followed by pictures with friends, invited guests and relatives.

After all the church activities, everyone proceeded to the reception ground. It was made up of speeches, music and dance. My wife's younger sister and her friends gave a fantastic dance presentation that thrilled the entire audience. One other exciting part of the wedding reception was the cutting of the cake which was done with much funfair and applause.

17. After the Wedding

After the wedding, we moved into the flat I shared with two older friends of mine, one was like an uncle to me. He had been very helpful to me financially and as a guide. The flat was a four bedroom flat, with two adjoining rooms separated by a large sitting room. The flat also had two toilets serving the two separate adjoining rooms.

When we got home after the wedding reception, we were both excited and glad that we were finally married after all the hurdles we had to cross to achieve this. I talked about this in greater detail earlier in this book.

We were excited that we were going to be together for the rest of our lives, but we were also very tired from all the activities that we had to go through from the wedding to the reception. Our loads of gifts had also been moved to our home, which we had to assemble in our room.

We got cleaned up, had our first dinner together as a couple. We chatted away, talking about all the day's experiences, laughed and made fun of the most exciting moments of the whole day. After all we went to bed and had the most peaceful sleep we have ever had in our lives.

18. The Moon Trip with Honey

The next three days was also full of fun and excitement. We had planned our honeymoon for three days and had booked a hotel in the center of town for this purpose. The whole goal was to spend time alone together from the rest of the world, have a long rest from all activities and have fun.

We had a great time together. We had long hours of sleep, woke up at any time we felt like, since we were not under pressure to meet any deadline or work.

We dressed up, with my wife wearing one of the most beautiful gowns I have ever seen her in. It was purple in colour, laced with shinning accessories and well fitted on her. She indeed looked very beautiful in it. And this dress remains lovely till this day.

We went to different restaurants to have our meals, took pictures together, visited places together and continue to chat ourselves away. It just seemed we should continue this forever.

We were still very much in fantasy island and didn't want reality to take us away from this moon trip, even though we were quite aware it had to come to an end sooner or later in fact just three days later.

By the third day, the moon trip with honey, was over and we were back to reality. We checked out of the hotel and headed back to our one room apartment.

Before we got married my wife had read lots of books about marriage, and she was armed with enough information of how to make marriage work. During the course of dating her she introduced me to some of these books and I read some, which were quite revealing.

Unlike now, back then I had not developed a strong desire and discipline for reading books. I had read just a few motivational and get rich books and was glowing in the excitement of what I found in them and when she introduced me to marriage books, I did not struggle to read them, because I knew what they were going to offer me, knew information, that will make me a better person and help our marriage.

As for my mother-in-law, to-day we are good friends. We chart, joke and have fun, together. She entertains me a great deal whenever I visit her home.

19. The Fruits of our Marriage

Our marriage is blessed with three beautiful daughers, namely:

- Angel Eunice Vincent, the first born.

- Joy Edomi Vincent, the second born.

- Anita Ohan Vincent, the third born.

They are sound in faith and character; hardworking and intelligent.

Daddy Loves You All.

ABOUT THE AUTHOR

Mr. Vincent Hope Okoh is a graduate of Mathematics Education and a very experienced Educator with over twenty (20) years of Teaching, Instructing and Training Experience.

He is an author of several academic and non-academic books among which are "My Leadership Collections", "The Story of My Mother", "10 Keys of How to Make Your Marriage Work", "Deeper Secrets of Wealth" etc.

He is an Entrepreneur, Management Expert and Leader, having lead his own company from an unknown position to an ICT firm of repute that has trained so many individuals in various ICT Skills, who are currently employed in different sectors of the economy.

He is happily married to Mrs. Deborah Nanchin Vincent and they are blessed with three beautiful daughters Angel, Joy and Anita.